AN

MW01254206

Following the GOLD

There is something for everyone in this delightful
new selection of verse by Bill Scott. There are poems
that tell of an age gone by, when bullock teams
hauled loads up hills as high as the heavens and
bushrangers roamed the Australian countryside.
There are stories of the sea and the saltbush, and tall
tales of dogs the size of ponies and gales that stir the
stars and put out the moon. There are soft, whimsical
poems about unicorns, dragons, porpoises and
bunyips, and laugh-out-loud ones about seasickness,
Martians and cowpats. This is a collection which
most appealingly conveys all the warmth, wisdom
and humour of one of Australia's best known and
loved men of letters.

For readers aged nine and over.

To the Brown Cat, Thick Fred and the Hairy Dog,
who helped

Following the GOLD

Bill Scott

AN OMNIBUS/PUFFIN BOOK

Omnibus Books
52 Fullarton Road
Norwood, South Australia 5067
Australia

Penguin Books Australia Ltd,
487 Maroondah Highway, P.O. Box 257,
Ringwood, Victoria 3134, Australia
Penguin Books Ltd,
Harmondsworth, Middlesex, England
Penguin Books,
40 West 23rd Street, New York, N.Y. 10010 U.S.A.
Penguin Books Canada Limited,
2801 John Street, Markham, Ontario, Canada L3R 1B4
Penguin Books (N.Z.) Ltd,
182–190 Wairau Road, Auckland 10, New Zealand

Published by Omnibus Books in association
with Penguin Books Australia Ltd 1989
Copyright © Bill Scott 1989
Illustrations copyright © Omnibus Books 1989

Typeset in Australia by Caxtons Pty Ltd, Adelaide
Made and printed in Australia by The Book Printer,
Maryborough, Victoria

CIP

Scott, Bill, 1923–
  Following the gold.

  ISBN 0 14 034006 8.

  1. Children's poetry, Australian. I. Title.
  (Series: Omnibus Puffin poetry).

A821′.3

Contents

Poems

Funny things
that need to be said
hang around
in the back of my head.

Beautiful words
and wild surprise
live in the poems
behind my eyes.

Frightening things,
terrors and fears
shiver in poems
between my ears.

There they sit
like a cloud of vapour.
They won't come out
on to the paper.

So, frustrated,
I sit and swear
at the poems that live
beneath my hair.

Let the Dragon Sleep

Our little town is a crumpled plate
                    balanced
on the back of a sleeping dragon.

He breathes in
            (cold of outer space)
                it's winter.

He breathes out
            (faint blue of bushfire smoke)
                suddenly it's summer.

The plate tilts to his slow
            heart   beat
and the tides run in

                    run out.

One century the dragon might stir,
            roll   over,
the plate of earth   t

                            u

                                m

                                    b

                                        l

                                            e

to infinite emptiness where no dragons are.

Hush, hush, be very gentle,
walk softly, don't wake him

let the dragon sleep.

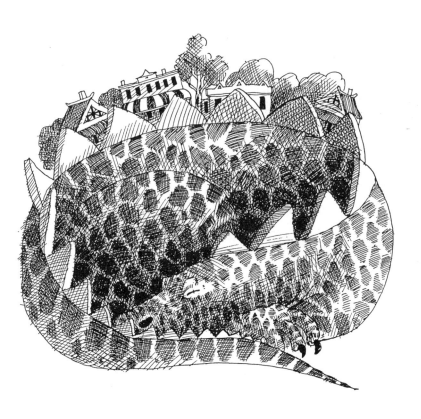

Thunderbolt

Thunderbolt came from the Hawkesbury River.
He was a bushranger, he was a rover.
Made all the rich folk shudder and shiver.
Wore fine clothes and lived in clover.
Riding high on a thoroughbred colt—
Bad man, bushranger, Thunderbolt.

Uralla, Armidale, Torrington as well,
Yarrowick Mountain where the farmers dwell
saw him ride, till a constable in blue
caught him and sent him to Cockatoo;
but he slipped from his cell and his iron chain
to wander free in the bush again.

He wandered far, he wandered wide.
Nobody knows just where he died
but on Yarrowick Mountain when the wind is high
and shadowy clouds go drifting by,
riding tall on his thoroughbred colt
comes the ghost of Thunderbolt.

Comes the ghost of Thunderbolt.

Bullock Teams

When I was a sapling boy
bullocks still pulled the timber jinkers.
Standing, they loomed solid as mountain chains.
When they moved they leaned into the yokes,
huge wheels turned slow, hubs screamed on axles.
The great logs followed them.

But at O'Mara's Hill, drivers tapped out their pipes,
took both hands to the whip.
The team dropped heads, backs levelled,
power poured from thrusting haunches—
they laid into it, Spot, Bally and Roger,
Blucher, Captain and patient Bob
so tug-chains rang like bells.

The logs tilted their ends to Heaven and
slow as funerals, helpless as corpses,
followed the team toward the screaming saws.

At the crest, the drivers paused to rest their cattle,
to fill and light their pipes and boil the billy.
Times were hard on bullocks and men in the timber.

It's all changed now.
I have found
you can pat and speak to a tractor all day
but it won't look round.

Rain in the Channel Country

To the swelling inland channels come the flighting
    ducks in multitudes
with pelicans in fleets that sail like schooners down
    the sky.
The black swans point their arrowheads toward
    the filling billabongs
and brolgas dance the breaking of the five-year dry.

Believe me, there are multitudes of acrobatic .
    parakeets
to celebrate the seeding of the grasses and
    the shrubs.
A screaming green and yellow mob that fossick in
    the tussock grass
or shriek and wheel in terror of the hawk that
    hangs above.

Fat frogs are burrowing upward from their time of
    sleep and burial,
silent under spiderwebs of cracked, eroded mud
till each pool has its complement.
                       Enthusiastic choristers
are croaking psalms of glory for the
    Diamantina flood.

Mangroves

On pitchy midnights mangroves wade
kneedeep like spiders through the mud.
On spindly roots they weave and stalk.

In sunlight, they are on parade—
you'd swear such anchored trees won't budge,
you'd say such silent trees don't talk . . .

When sun and moon are sunk below
the curved horizon of the sea
like stealthy animals they creep.

Don't ask me where it is they go
or what they do so secretly
like spiders hunting there, kneedeep.

I'm sure I wouldn't want to know
what evil words tree says to tree
when all good things are sunk in sleep.

But, if you wake close to the sea
on blowing nights of wind and rain
and twigs scratch on your windowpane

don't call for help from me—
                              from me.

The Spiny Ant-eater's Song

A porpoise lived on a mountain top.
He said, "Well, bless my eye!
There's only trees, there aren't any seas.
I'm bored and hungry and dry.

"I'll roll downhill to the river brim
and follow it to the shore
where the breakers beat and there's fish to eat
and I'll never come back no more!"

He swam and swam by river and dam,
downhill all the way
when out of the blue hopped a kangaroo,
going the other way.

"Where are you going, old kangaroo,
bouncing along like a ball?
There's nothing up there but grass and air
and trees where the mopokes call!"

"I come from the beach," said the kangaroo,
"where my tail was never dry.
I'm going to hop to a mountain top
and live up there in the sky.

"Away from the hawk and the mollymawk
and the grey seas breaking wet.
I'll take my ease beneath the trees
and forget the foam and fret."

Now the porpoise rolls over sea-green shoals
and the kangaroo sleeps quite dry.
Both of them sing like anything
while the rest of the world rolls by.

So, children, if you're a kangaroo
don't try to live in the foam,
and if you're a porpoise, take my word
a hill can never be home.

If you're a possum, get off the ground
and curl in a friendly tree.
The happiest animals you will find
all live where they ought to be.

Poem For My Children

From Sydney Cove
they all set sail,
a doctor and a sailor
and a boy to bail.
Out through the Heads
and sailing south
little *Tom Thumb*
left the harbour mouth.

Tom Thumb pitched,
Tom Thumb rolled,
the sea-wind blew
and they all got cold.
They all got wet
with flying spray
as little *Tom Thumb*
sailed southaway.

They came to a beach
and stepped ashore.
The boy didn't have
to bail any more.
They dried their clothes
and made new friends
where the south coast starts
and the east coast ends.

Then back to sea
and sailing home,
safe to Sydney,
wet with foam.
A boy to bail,
a doctor and his chum,
not forgetting
little *Tom Thumb*.

The Lighthouse Keeper and the Herring Gull

The lighthouse keeper sat on a rock and a sad, salt
    tear wept he.
"I'm tired of biscuits and tins of beef, I want a fish
    for tea!
But I haven't a hook and I haven't a line to throw in
    the salty sea."

He peered to the east where the breakers broke,
    he blinked his teary eye.
He looked behind where his tower rose like a
    steeple in the sky
And he saw a wise old herring gull perched on a
    rock close by.

Said the keeper, "A gull has an easy time when he
    wants a fish to swallow.
He rises up till he spies a shoal where the billows
    bellow hollow.
He dives down deep and he gulps a fish, with
    another one to follow."

The keeper found a rusty nail and hammered it into
    a hook;
He ravelled a string both long and strong from his
    cosy sea-boot sock;
He baited the line and cast it in with a crafty,
    hungry look.

He caught a whiting and a bream, he almost
   caught a whale,
He hooked a crab by its big, round claws and a
   flathead by the tail
And he tossed each fish behind him, where they fell
   in an old tin pail.

Then he snavelled a shark that broke his line. He
   didn't really care.
He had fish enough to fry for tea, and for breakfast,
   and to spare,
And even enough for the herring gull that he
   thought deserved a share.

So he turned around to view his catch with shouts
   of joy and mirth,
But his roar of rage at what he saw was heard from
   Cairns to Perth—
An empty pail, and the fullest, fattest herring gull
   on earth.

The Lion and the Unicorn

Once upon a time, a long time ago
lived a unicorn with a spike on his nose.
He had opal eyes and a coat like moonlight,
he could run so fast his shadow couldn't catch him
till he stopped.

He was lovely to look at, but oh! He was nasty!
He'd wait till the others were sleeping soundly,
creep up quietly so they didn't waken
and prod them on the backside with his
    pointy spike.
"WOW!!!" they shouted.

Kangaroos leapt and wallabies bellowed.
Wombats dug so he couldn't reach them.
Possums stayed in the tops of gum trees,
snakes and lizards hid among boulders
while the unicorn giggled and sharpened his spike
on sandstone.

One day unicorn was running up a mountain.
Under a clump of crimson waratah
he saw a fat, round, furry backside
and heard the sound of somebody snoring
very loudly.

He crept as quiet as a mouse over feathers,
jabbed, then laughed at the yell that followed.
Out of the bushes, faster than a rocket
sprang a huge marsupial lion.
It ate him!

But the lion was not as clever as he thinked . . .
both him and the unicorn are now extinct.

A Way to Get Rid of Bunyips

The Blue Lake Bunyip
chased a dog.
The dog ran to hide
and the hide made some leather
and the leather made a plait
and the plait made a whip
and the whip made a crack
and the crack made a leak
in the bottom of the lake
so the lake dried up
and so did the bunyip.
And the bunyip turned to
thistledown, thistledown;
blow on the thistledown,
bunyip's gone.

Three Fleas

Here's three fleas with muscular knees
who can leap as high as the tallest trees.
BOING. BOING. BOING!

This is the mouse with a thoughtful frown
who was home for the fleas when they settled down;
three little fleas with powerful knees
who could leap as high as the tallest trees.
BOING. BOING. BOING!

This is the dingo, hungry and brown
who gobbled the mouse with the thoughtful frown
who was home for the fleas with powerful knees
who could jump as high as the tallest trees—
(guess where the fleas have gone?)

This is the man with the wrinkled forehead
who trapped the dingo, hungry and brown
who gobbled the mouse who was home to the fleas,
three little fleas with powerful knees
(guess where the fleas are now?)

This is the bunyip, green and horrid
who gulped the man with the wrinkled forehead
who trapped the dingo hungry and brown
who gobbled the mouse with the thoughtful frown
who was home for the fleas when the sun went
    down—
three little fleas with powerful knees
who could leap as high as the tallest trees
with ease.

A bunyip who is a nasty sight,
whose hair and whiskers are turning white,
who wriggles and scratches and kicks and bites
because he can't get any sleep at nights—
there are fleas that worry and fleas that tease,
three little fleas with muscular knees
who can leap as high as the tallest trees
and change their home with the greatest of ease—

You know where the fleas are now!!

Circus

Hustle, hustle, my friend Russell,
here comes a leopard, all spots and muscle
following a crocodile playing on a whistle.

Scurry, scurry, my friend Murray,
here comes a tiger in a terrible hurry
following a leopard all spots and muscle
following a crocodile playing on a whistle
following Russell.

Fly like a fairy, my friend Mary,
here comes a hairy drom-e-dary
following a tiger in a terrible hurry
following a leopard, all spots and muscle
following a crocodile playing on a whistle
following Russell.

Don't be lazy, my friend Daisy,
here's a gorilla, all wild and crazy
following a hairy dromedary
following a tiger in a terrible hurry
following a leopard all spots and muscle
following a crocodile playing on a whistle
following Russell.

Then a policeman shouted,
"ALL TURN ROUND!!"

Then Daisy and Mary and Murray and Russell
followed the crocodile playing on his whistle
following the leopard, all spots and muscle
following the hairy dromedary
following the tiger in a terrible hurry
and the giant gorilla with a charming smile . . .
All dancing to the music of the crocodile.

Old Hen

I had an old hen with a bright red beak
who laid me seventeen eggs a week.
Last Tuesday morning she fell on her side,
caught the measles and went and died.

Poor old hen! I was terribly sad
when I thought of the eggs I hadn't had
but since she was gone I thought I should
use her remains as best I could.

I took her feathers and washed them clean
and stitched some cloth on my sewing-machine
to make a pillow where I lay my head
when sundown comes and I go to bed.

Her tail made a duster for the furniture,
to clean the ornaments and sweep the floor.
I used her feet with a satisfied screech
to scratch my back where my arms won't reach.

I couldn't think of anything to do with her comb
but I used her beak to write this pome.
Her little bits and pieces went to feed the cat
and I cooked the rest and that was that.

I ate that old hen, all juicy and brown
and later on, when my dinner went down
I pulled her wishbone, won, and then
wished myself another old hen.

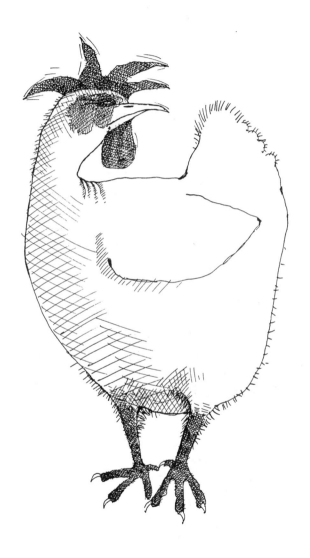

Over the Waves

Goodbye Melbourne! The ship's away
gliding gently through Port Phillip Bay,
we're off to Tasmania. Hip hooray!
aboard the Bass Strait Ferry.

Through the Rip and out to sea
where big blue waves roll endlessly;
(I'm sorry I had that pie for tea
with a bottle of sarsaparilla!)

The wind is tugging the masthead flag,
the bows go up in the air, then sag.
Quickly! Hand me a plastic bag
aboard the bloochie oooriaghhhhh ptoooo.

The ship rolls low, the ship rolls high,
the passengers whoop and heave and cry—
they lean on the rails and hope to die
Aboard aaaaarghlie. Herrrrrrp!

Safely in Launceston, feeling no pain,
we're going home in an aeroplane.
We'll never go back to sea again
on board the Bass Strait Ferry!

Crab Hunting

Slime around the ankles,
slither to the knees—
we go crabbing through
the mangrove trees.
Thick black soft mud,
Oh! Gee! Pooh!
Knee deep, squish, thud,
(there goes a shoe).
Where has Sandra gone?
Did she trip?
Here she comes now—
sludge, pong, drip.
Here's the path out,
it's not too far.
We'll have to hose her down before
we let her in the car!
Quick, turn the water on,
rub, scrub, do.
See the slush all washing off—
Stink! Pong! Pooh!

Thick Green Slime

Greasy eels slide in it
bullyfrogs hide in it
old fish died in it,
thick green slime.
Cane toads call in it
rotten logs sprawl in it
people fall in it,
thick green slime.
Guinea pigs bog in it
fingernails clog in it
there's a dead dog in it,
thick green slime.
Mosquitoes sing in it
leeches cling in it
sandflies sting in it,
thick green slime.
Look where Bertie is,
look where Gertie is.
Filthy dirty is
thick green slime.

Grandpa and the Martian

The Martian oozed up our garden path
and rang the front door bell;
his scales were blue, his teeth were green,
he had a horrible smell.

"What do you want?" asked Grandpa.
"You'd better not come inside,
you'd ruin all the carpets and
the scatter rugs besides."

The Martian lowered his spacesuit
to the ground with a rattling clank.
"Have you got any second-hand chewing gum
to mend my oxygen tank?

"I'm losing all my pressure through
this rusty little leak
and I need to plug it as quick as I can,"
he said with a plaintive squeak.

Grandpa ran to the bedroom.
From under the reading lamp
he grabbed some last night's chewing gum
that was sticky still, and damp.

He handed it to the Martian
who took it with a shout
and plastered it over the leaky bit
where the gas was whistling out.

Then Captain Chook, the Martian,
went safely home to Mars,
where the little moons spin like humming tops
among the silent stars.

Now Grandpa often tells the tale
while sipping at his rum;
how he saved the expedition
with some second-hand chewing gum.

The Little Green Man

The flying saucer landed,
a little green man came out.
His head was wild and leafy
like a giant Brussels sprout.

He wandered across the paddock
to where the old horse fed;
and, "Take me to your leader!"
the little green man said.

The horse was hard of hearing,
his sight was growing dim.
He didn't think of little green men,
it was just a bush to him—

One bite, one chew, one swallow;
(it doesn't bear thinking on)!
Now the saucer rusts in the field alone
but the little green man has gone.

Splat

Young Aubrey was out
in the paddock, hoeing,
in a dream, not looking
where he was going;
chipping along
his woolgathering way,
head in the clouds
and nothing to say,
when he suddenly slipped
and fell on his back,
hitting the ground
an awful smack.

He looked at the seat
of his pants with a sigh.
"I see that a cow
has just passed by!"

Lazy Jack

We were working out on the western plains,
   building a section of road,
Kilometres from the nearest pub or anyone's abode;
Not even a shearing shed in sight, not even a
   wayside shack,
And the sleepiest man in all the gang was a bloke
   named Lazy Jack.

He moved as slow as a fossil, in fact. He barely
   moved at all.
(Except he could go like lightning when he heard
   the "Smoke-oh!" call.)
Then he'd speed to the nearest patch of shade and
   sprawl out like a lizard,
And the only way we could wake him up was to
   poke him in the gizzard.

One day at lunchtime Jack looked round to find a
   shady tree—
But there were no trees around that place as far as
   the eye could see.
The rest of us ate our lunch in the sun and swore at
   the traffic controller,
And nobody noticed Lazy Jack creep under the big
   road roller.

Nobody thought to wake him up. Nobody noticed
  him go
Till a couple of seconds after we started we heard a
  kind of "Ohhhhh!",
A sort of muffled popping sound. By then it was
  too late
For there was Jack, spread out on the road as flat as
  a dinner plate.

The foreman looked and scratched his neck and
  said in a thoughtful way,
"We'll never get *him* in a coffin! We'd be scraping
  here all day!
I'll tell you what—we'll back up a truck and drop a
  load of rubble,
Then grade it out and roll it flat. It'll save a lot of
  trouble!"

That's what we did. There's a lonely cross out there
  on the empty plain,
Three hundred metres from Jackson's fence just
  after you pass the drain.
But the traffic controller, the ganger and me, and
  all the rest of the men
Will never forget poor Lazy Jack. Or eat raspberry
  jelly again.

The Queensland Dog

A stranger came from New South Wales, and he
    was tall and brown.
He lined beside us at the bar, he sank his schooners
    down,
And all the while, to pass the time, he told us
    doubtful tales
Of the country he laid claim to—remarkable
    New South Wales.

With soil so rich and fertile, so ran his line of talk,
That pumpkin vines fair sprinted along, as fast as a
    man could walk.
He said it took two hours, sometimes, to ride
    through the hollow logs
For the timber grew so thick and tall. And then he
    mentioned dogs.

Little Maginnis spoke up then, arising from
    his seat.
"I dunno about them other things, but at dogs
    we've got you beat.
I was boundary riding once," he said, "on a station
    Longreach way
And lost me bearings among the hills, right at the
    end of the day.

"So I let the old moke poke along and find his own
  way in the dark
Until in the distance I saw a light. And then I heard
  him bark.
Well, station dogs are mostly noise. I never took
  no heed.
I only wanted me bearings, and I could have done
  with a feed.
So I went on riding toward the light, just following
  me nose,
And then I heard him bark again, but this time he's
  up close.

"I needn't have worried, he's only a dog, the kind
  cow cockies keep
That chase the dingoes away at night, then lay all
  day and sleep.
When he gets nearer he whines a bit, friendly, quiet
  and deep.
Then he stands on his hind legs to lick me face, and
  I see his gentle eye,
And his dusty coat and wagging tail by the
  starlight in the sky—
And the horse I was sitting on at the time was
  seventeen hands high."

The stranger paled, and admitted, with the wind
  took out of his sails,
That dogs grow bigger in Queensland than they do
  in New South Wales.

The Dog's Ghost Story

An ancient, grey-muzzled drover's dog
lay in the shade of a weatherboard shack
and told the admiring dogs of the town
how life is lived on the lonely, brown
stock routes of the Great Outback.

"Give me the life of a drover's dog,
not that of a pampered city pet
when the grass is green in the early Spring,
the hobbles clink and the blowflies sing,
(I can hear their music yet).

"We started once from Waverley Gate
with seventeen thousand crossbred ewes.
By Nardoo and Wanaaring town
we followed the Paroo River down.
'Twas the safest track to use.

"By Nocoleche and Chinaman's Bore,
by Yanta Bangie and Mandalay,
by Coona Coona and Bunker's Tank
till we came at last to the Darling bank
at the end of the dusty day,

"We settled them down on the bare, flat plain
above the Darling waterholes.
'There's wind in that sunset!' the drover said
as he peered at the mares-tails overhead
the colour of campfire coals.

"'There's wind in that sky!' he said again,
'and I wish we were safe at home!'
As though he knew an enormous breeze
had stripped the Flinders Ranges' trees
and was headed across Lake Frome.

"I've seen some wind-storms in my time
that stirred the stars and put out the moon
but this was a real Wilcannia Shower—
a hurricane of enormous power
like a China Seas typhoon.

"The front of it reached us just on dawn.
By the time we could see in the murky light
the ground was moving under our feet
as the surface stirred in a solid sheet
and the horses screamed in fright.

"'Now, Towser,' the drover yelled to me,
'It's time you earned your crimson feed!
It's the testing time for dog and man.
Get round the flank as fast as you can
and try to steady the lead!'

"I passed the mob with the wind behind
but when I got there and tried to slow
I hadn't a chance. That Wilcannia Shower
was doing a thousand miles an hour—
then it really began to blow.

"With choking dust so thick in the sky
and below the mob, we suddenly found
we were walking around, no trouble or care,
about five hundred feet in the air
as though it was solid ground.

"But safe enough, on that thickened dust—
(I tell the tale, though it may seem strange).
We headed east for some pleasant spot
with feed and water; but we forgot
the GREAT DIVIDING RANGE.

"Just south of Tamworth, near Goonoo Goonoo,*
this aeroplanic convoy stalled.
There's a great big dent in the ranges there,
no trees—just rock, all slippery bare.
Greasy Gully, it's called,

"Where seventeen thousand flying ewes,
forty dogs, and a cook named Bess,
thirty horses, eleven men,
two bags of flour and a Morris Ten
made one enormous mess.

"That was years ago, but the locals swear
(with staring eyeballs and skins that creep)
some nights there's a noise like two trains meeting
in a vat of grease, and the horrid bleating
of raspberry-jam-like sheep."

*(pronounced gúnner-gernóo)

The township dogs swore admiring swears
but a dog that belonged to a farmer bloke
said, "How did you escape their plight?"
"I didn't," he said. "I was killed outright!"
Then he vanished away.

        Like smoke.

A Cheeky Bushranger

(7 January 1869)

Along the Maryborough Road
stopping every stranger
Detective Smyth and a Constable
hunted a bad bushranger
who had robbed the Gympie mail coach
so daring and so bold
and stolen *Mister Freeston's watch*
as well as the miner's gold.

Detective Smyth and the Constable
in his oilskin covered hat
discovered a rider among the trees
not far from Durramboi Flat.
The bushranger waved to Detective Smyth
who called upon him to "STAND!!!"
then drew his big revolver out
and shot himself through the hand.

The Constable lifted his carbine up,
took aim, and pulled the trigger,
(though exactly where the bullet went
no one could ever figure).
The bushranger lifted his hat to them
and wished them a pleasant day
then turned his race horse into the bush
and cantered slowly away.

Moonlight

Jill, Jill, climb high on the hill,
the moon has risen, it's standing still.
High, high in a milky sky,
a golden orange, an owl's eye.
Call for a cloud to come for a shroud
to hide from sight that golden light
before it sees us, stoops to freeze us
and carries us off to where white stars
spangle the sky like frost on grass.

Jill, Jill, run down from the hill,
the rocks are standing black and still.
Crickets are shrilling, the dark is chill.

Come down.
Come down to the scattered town,
to the firelit room where embers glow.
Come in from the moon, be safe below
the cold slopes of standing stone.

Blankets warm and windows tight
is the best place for a winter night.

Blind Girl

They say I am in darkness. I have heard
them speak of light that I shall never see.
They tell me of the brilliance of a bird.
Crimson and gold. The words sound sweet enough
upon the air, but what are words to me?

Standing beneath this pillar called a tree,
this somehow friendly roughness I can touch,
I hear the birdsong falling wistfully
through the soft air toward my waiting ear.
Shall I miss gold or crimson overmuch?

For what is dark, when you have seen no light
And what is colour but an empty word?
Clasping this bark I stand in endless night
Hearing the wind move greenly through the
     leaves.
Hearing the gentle grieving of the bird.

Shy Grey Ghost

Little grey ghost in the corner of my room
hiding away with the mop
and the broom,
once in the dark I heard you cry—
wispy as spiderwebs,
soft and shy.

Won't you come out from behind the door?
Please don't be afraid any more,
sad little ghost at the bedroom end
how would you like
to be my friend?

Sorry I gave you such a fright.
I get lonely too,
at night.
Don't be sad, I understand.
If you're frightened you can hold my hand.

We'll be together. You can stay
till morning brings
another day.
We'll tell stories till the clock strikes three
and I'll love you
if you love me.

Shy grey ghost at my bedroom end,
don't go away.
I need a friend.

Cats

Cats ride with witches,
snap like mousetraps,
creep like water.

Cats sit high, peer downward,
chatter at birds and spit at dogs.
They keep the bargain they have made
with other cats,
wrestle and scream on roofs,
thrash in the flower-beds,
moan like ghosts from fence-tops
spring like tigers
yet, somehow, kittens come . . .

Cats droop asleep, are warm on winter nights,
their coats spit sparks in the dry windy weather.
Self-contained as trees they watch their humans
and are not easily blandished.
Cats insist where dogs suggest . . .

Yet it is no house
where no cat sits at fireside.

People are kept by cats.

Frogs

for Elizabeth Scott

Fat frogs squat greenly
in waterholes.
Swim with hind legs
on hinges.

They sleep all day
under tank-stands
where damp fern fronds
hang in fringes.

But on blowy nights
when rain rattles
on the stiff leaves
of palm and mango,

They swell their throats,
bellow, honk and tinkle—
that's what I call
a frog fandango.

50

A Dog's Life

All around me the suburbs are sleeping,
the houses are silent and dark.
The traffic is dead. There's a moon overhead
and the bandicoots grub in the park.

It's a quarter past three in the morning
in the yard I have under my care—
but a shadowy Stranger lurks in the hydrangea
and thinks I don't know that it's there.

I can sense there's a Spook in the bushes
or a Shadow from under a stone—
despite Its pretences It's inside my fences
and I know that It's after my bone!

So I up and I shout, "Bloody murder!
Get out of the bushes, you Thing!
Get your eyes off my bone! Just leave it alone
or I'll chew both your ankles to string!"

My screaming cuts right through the silence
and wakes all my mates round about.
They leap to their feet all the length of the street
and lift up their voices, and shout!

Then there's cursing from black bedroom windows
and hurling of sandshoes and balls.
We roar on uncaring of shouting and swearing
as missiles bounce off kennel walls.

The Ghost huddles deep in the bushes,
afraid of the tumult and noise.
I cuddle my bone in the darkness alone
and am grateful to all of the boys.

As the last yelp dies down in the distance
and slumber resumes its dark reign
my vigil I'm keeping. As soon as they're sleeping
I'll do it all over again!

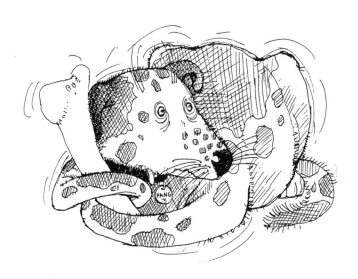

Mind Your Language

Possums are cheerful. Possums aren't glum,
they yell all night from the top of the gum
saying bad things. I'm glad, in a way,
I don't understand what possums say.

They use bad language when the sky is black.
Other possums answer them and swear right back.
They know what they're saying is wicked
    and wrong
but possums are cheerful and swear right along.

When they die they won't be forgiven.
I'm not sure where they'll go.
It won't be Heaven . . .

Beach Dogs

Gritty sand and sunshine in front of the dunes
where sea-wind and water sing their own strange
    tunes;
people and dogs in a great congregation,
every shape and size and colour, tribe and nation.
All mixing happily and nobody minds—
big ones and little ones—you meet all kinds.

Chasing flocks of seabirds to wheel in the blue,
waiting for chop bones at the barbecue;
splashing through the eddies after terns and
    noddies
and shaking icy water over sunbathing bodies.
Racing over tablecloths with friends in pursuit,
tipping bottles over, sitting in the fruit.
Sand in the sandwiches, sand in the cake,
sand in the water where the combers break.

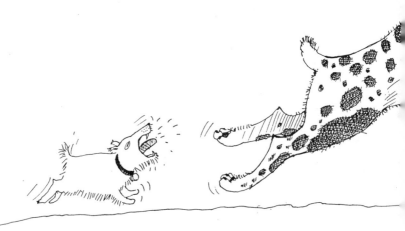

Sprinting through the beach vines, hurdling over
   stones,
munching thoughtfully on last week's chicken
   bones,
helping fishermen, knocking children down—
It's a lot more fun on the beach than in town.

People and dogs in a great congregation,
every colour, shape and size, every nation
all mixed together and nobody minds—
big ones and little ones. You meet all kinds.

Ruff

Behold this dog, his name is Ruff.
His coat is tangled, matted stuff.
His owner said (and this is true),
"It is as if he'd rolled in glue
then flung his body in some weird
exploded Santa Claus's beard!"

The mystery is that though he sheds
masses of fur on chairs and beds,
carpets, car seats and the floor,
he stays as hairy as before.
Though, when asleep, his forelegs twitch
it's hard to tell which end is which
or know, by exercise of sight
which end is wag, which end is bite.

His jaws droop a perpetual grin,
his forelock reaches to his chin
through which his eyes peer hopefully
at fence and lamp post, shrub and tree.
He stands to drink; the slurping sound
is heard for many metres round;
he shakes his head, dispensing showers,
his beard stays wet for hours and hours
and to put callers at their ease
he places it upon their knees.
Not very bright but pretty tough
is my acquaintance, name of Ruff.

Kittens

for Janette Wilcox

Wrestle and jump, wrestle and jump,
spring on your sister and land with a bump.
Hustle and wrestle and ambush your brother,
scurry and chase from one room to the other,
that's how it is with kittens.

Quiver and pounce, quiver and pounce,
stiffen your unsteady legs and bounce.
Spread out the fur on your back like a sail,
spring on your mother and murder her tail.
That's how it is with kittens.

Pummel and purr, pummel and purr,
wrap yourselves up in one big ball of fur.
For a little while sleep, and dream of a mouse.
Suddenly there is peace in the house.
That's how it is with kittens.

scritch
scratch
file
file

Siamese Cats

Siamese cats are a peril.
They do just about what they please.
They vanish when wanted, of course.
Their eyes shine like moons of blue beryl.
Their voices are raucous and hoarse
with pride that they are Siamese.

They favour black masks, like bushrangers.
They seem fairly nervous of rats.
They leap on the stomachs of sleepers.
They ladder the stockings of strangers
like cinnamon-hued Jack-the-Rippers.

Some say they are not really cats!

The Old Man's Song

When I was a young man I followed the gold,
deep in a mineshaft, all muddy and cold.
Deep in the dark with a flickering light
and never a nugget to gladden my sight.
But it's way, hey ! Now I am old,
the mornings were silver, the sunsets were gold.

When I was a young man I followed the sea,
cold, wet and shivering often I'd be.
Rocked in the crows-nest or rolled down below
or sweating my soul out where the Gulf traders go.
But it's way, hey ! Now I am old
the oceans were sapphires, the beaches were gold.

Now I am an old man I sit in the sun
thinking and dreaming of things that I've done.
Remembering laughter, forgetting the pain
and I'd go out and do it all over again.
For it's way, hey ! Lift it along,
what good is your life if it isn't a song?

About the Author

Bill Scott is often referred to, affectionately, as one of Australia's grand old men of letters. He has been involved with books, as author, bookseller, editor and publisher, for over thirty years, and has been working as a full-time writer since 1974. His literary output includes novels, short stories, verse, biographies, magazine articles, anthologies and songs, and his poetry and short stories have been widely anthologised.

Bill was born in Bundaberg, Queensland. He served four years in the Royal Australian Navy (1942–46) and has worked as a seaman, a steam-engine driver, a prospector and a miner. His interests—prospecting, wood-carving and folklore—reflect his colourful background.

Bill is now a grandfather of four. He and his wife (author Mavis Scott) live on the Darling Downs, about 150 kilometres from Brisbane.